The Child Care Director's Guide

to

Building Culture

39 Strategies for Child Care Directors to Build a Positive and Productive Workplace

By: Stephanie Harris, M. Ed.

ISBN: 978-1-64775-059-6

Contact the Author

Email: StephanieM.Ed12@gmail.com

www.ChildCareEmpowered.com

Thank You!

Whether you purchased this book for yourself or came across it some other way, I would like to take a moment to say thank you for your commitment to the early childhood education field.

As you dive into the content, you may have questions or even feedback or ideas. I invite you to share them with me and others in the early childhood community by joining our free group 'Child Care Empowered' on Facebook or by emailing at StephanieM.Ed12@gmail.com

Happy Reading!

Preface

Two things happened that led me to write this book. (1.) I taught in a school where a lack of building leadership drained the life out of some of the most committed teachers that I've ever met and (2.) I met my lifelong goal, at 26 years old, of opening a childcare center only to have my center license (and subsequently my dream) put in jeopardy because of my own poor leadership.

It's always amazing when we take a moment to pause and gain a refreshing realization that our challenges and struggles occurred only to catapult us to the next level of success. Perhaps your struggles, whether they be related to staffing, enrollment, or needy parents, are occurring to gently push you towards the level of success that you've dreamed of.

To my current team and those who have moved on - thank you. Every single experience, good or bad, served a purpose and helped me to grow.

"And we know that **all things** work together for good to those who love God, to those who are called according to His purpose."

Romans 8:28

Introduction

I fell in love with my team by accident. My newly promoted Director (and *friend* of ten years) left early and never came back after an incident involving jury duty. Here I was with 20 employees and nearly 100 kids and was left with no other choice but to lead. I had started some work on culture a few months before her departure but I suddenly realized that I would have to go into culture building overdrive if I was going to effectively lead the school on my own. The culture shift that resulted from this moment changed the trajectory of my business and changed everything about how I lead. For that, I am thankful.

In the pages to come, I'll be sharing strategies for developing a positive, healthy, and happy workplace culture that you and your team love. Undoubtedly, workplace culture is one of the most unexplored concepts by leaders in our industry. However, once explored and addressed, culture will be the single most important key to success.

Entrepreneur David Cummings describes workplace culture as, "the only sustainable competitive advantage completely within the control of the entrepreneur." This is great news! Not only will an improved workplace culture give you an advantage over your competition but it's also within your control, meaning **you have the power to create a healthy culture** that leads your program to success. You deserve to go to a work environment that you love every day - and so does your team. Get ready to make a shift.

Happy Culture Building!

Part I: The Foundation

When building any physical structure, contractors generally begin by pouring in a foundation that is designed to last the test of time. The structure rests on the foundation and is protected against moisture, cold air, and even shifts in the earth around it. As you work to build an amazing child care program, an important question comes to mind - what foundation is your team resting on?

As child care program leaders, a ton of us work from our heart. Many of us get into the field because of our love for children unbeknownst to the challenges that the adults will present. We naively believe that if we give people the rules and treat them kindly, everything will go smoothly. We also don't often realize that in addition to managing people, we're also responsible for managing the people's work environment. This is where culture kicks in. Organizations each have a unique personality and employee culture is at its root. As leaders it is our responsibility to define the culture for our program and to also ensure that the decisions made within our program support the culture that we've defined.

Before we introduce culture building strategies, there are a few key factors that we need to point out.

1. Every person is not YOUR person. This includes both staff and parents. The truth is that not everyone is a good 'fit' for your program's philosophy. As a leader, it is your responsibility to send people on their way when they are not a good fit in order to preserve the integrity of your program philosophy and your overall philosophy as a leader.

2. Being good in the classroom is not enough. There are some great teachers who aren't great employees and team members. Be prepared to pass on great teachers who lack the character and core values that your program is built upon.

3. A culture has been established in your workplace, even if it wasn't you (or your company's leaders) who established it. The great news is that YOU are in control of your company's culture and have the power to make changes that will shift the trajectory of your team and child care program.

4. Whether you've been in business for years, or you're just starting out, you'll be able to use our strategies to create a culture that makes both you and your team happy to go to work each day.

For the purpose of this book, we define culture as the actual pattern of behaviors that exist within your program and the shared belief of what behaviors are normal **and** tolerated within your organization. In its most simple state, culture is the work environment that's been established in your program. It is the answer to questions like, how do I get my staff to come to work? How can I get staff to work together? How do I reduce turnover? How can I get buy-in from staff? How do I increase morale? How do I get people to follow our policies and protocol? Culture is not just one thing, it is a combination of many things that all work together to establish norms for your program.

Now that we've gotten that out of the way, let's get to the strategies :)

STRATEGY 1:

Develop a Hiring System

(aka Employee Wait List)

It goes without saying that staffing is generally the greatest problem that child care owners and directors face. For quite some time the primary challenge for our industry has been maintaining staff and keeping turnover low. More recently, however, this focus has shifted to include the challenge of simply finding staff who want to work. A quick search on any hiring website will highlight the enormous demand for child care program staff, making it easy for employees to leave your company and move on to the next if your culture doesn't give them a reason to stay. Unfortunately, when people leave, we have to replace them quickly in order to meet regulatory requirements for ratio which means that time is of the essence.

One of the easiest ways for child care program leaders to be proactive is to develop an employee wait list. This is a list of potential employees who are familiar with your program and who you can reach out to with ease. This hiring strategy requires that you build an electronic list of applicants, market to the list, and use the list regularly.

Building the List: Have every applicant complete an online pre-screening application that captures their name, email address, phone number, years of experience, asking pay, and allows them to provide a written response to the tell me about yourself question. *Google forms* is a free online tool that will allow you to create the online application and all responses are captured in a single spreadsheet for you to reference in the future.

Marketing to the List: Once you've created your list, you should regularly email them with employment openings as well as newsletters that capture why your program is a great place to work. MailChimp is a free online tool that will allow you to send out mass emails but also allows recipients to unsubscribe if they are no longer interested in employment. The goal is to develop a following so that you remain in the back of their mind when their employment situation changes. Remember, even if they are not your ideal candidate, they may refer others who are seeking employment in the field!

Out of the Box Idea: Group Interviews

There's nothing more frustrating than scheduling a day's worth of interviews and having only one or two people actually show up. This can put a huge damper on your day and also severely set back your hiring timeline. Group interviews are a great alternative and reduce the impact of no-show applicants. Our program may invite as many as 30 people to a group interview (although we've never had all 30 show up). Applicants are not aware of the group interview format until they actually arrive. During the interview, applicants sit in a circle and respond to the interview questions which are asked verbally. In addition to saving a ton of time, group interviews also allow you to see an applicant's interpersonal skills in action.

STRATEGY 2:
Know Your Top 10

If you've ever attended an empowerment workshop, you've probably heard all about the benefits of writing down your goals. Writing things down not only provides some basic accountability, but also serves as a self-reflection tool that clears your mind for higher level thinking. All program leaders have thoughts of their ideal employee somewhere in their mind but have you taken the time to write out a specific list exactly what you want in your employees?

Create a list of the top 10 things you want in an employee. Consider things like attitude, attendance, understanding of child development, etc. Your current employees may not have all of these things now but with the right culture, you may be able to coach and develop them in the areas where they need growth.

STRATEGY 3:
Establish Core Values

Every organization needs an authentic framework that defines what the company values most. This is why core values are so important. Core values serve as the foundation for making decisions (especially those related to hiring and firing), and promote consistency throughout your program. This consistency allows your staff to go from thinking 'I do' to 'We do' which helps them to grab hold of your center and take ownership of it. In other words, core values help give your company a sense of identity.

Core values should be authentic to your organization and who you are as leader which is why I recommend avoiding creating core values as a team. In addition to being posted centrally, staff should be trained on your core values and held accountable to them if you want them to serve an actual purpose. The values should also be varied enough to touch different facets of your expectations but also simple enough to memorize.

The core values for my program are made up of four elements that embody exactly who we are individually and collectively and who we want on our team:

- ***Customer Focused*** which addresses how we serve our children and families.
- ***Integrity*** which addresses good character and fully following policies and regulations.
- ***Positivity & Enthusiasm*** which addresses attitude and interactions.
- ***Have Fun!*** Which addresses our work environment as well as personal care and development.

Although the core values in my program aren't tangible, they can be felt in the atmosphere at our program. One of the biggest compliments that we receive from prospective parents who've toured our center stating they can feel the love, passion, or positivity of our staff which I believe is a direct result of our core values.

Choose core values for your program. Ideally, you'll want to create no more than 5 or 6 so that they remain meaningful. You can find a ton of examples by looking at the about section of almost any big corporation or you may find the list below to be helpful.

STRATEGY 4:
Review your Vision, Mission and Philosophy

The vision, mission, and philosophy of your program help to shape your culture by giving your company direction. Once you've determined your goals and purpose, be sure to hire people who can align to each. Some companies take it a step further with an education pledge to parents or creed of service. Be careful not to create too many statements to live by as this can cause them to lose their value and become decorative posters on the walls of your school that lack any genuine following. If your vision, mission, and philosophy statements are to have an impact on your culture, your people have to be aware of them, believe in them, and use them as their guide as long as they are on your team.

- **Vision Statement:** The desired future position of the company.
- **Mission Statement:** What the company was formed to do.
- **Philosophy Statement:** The company's approach to education, parent relationships, and care of children.

Strategy 5: Employee Scorecards

There is a huge desire for transparency and feedback within the workplace. A transparent culture not only empowers employees but also adds an invaluable sense of credibility and trustworthiness. This trust is especially important in our industry since we are responsible for the safety and well being of the children in our care. Employee scorecards are a great way to know where every one of your employees stand. Scorecards are less formal than performance evaluations and point out specific things to work on in the short-term rather than at the end of the year. When used appropriately, scorecards can help problems to be solved faster and help employees achieve higher levels of performance. They also force leaders to provide regular feedback and support a culture of continuous improvement and growth.

We recommend setting a program wide quality focus and using scorecards to measure progress towards a common goal. In addition, scorecards work best when employees self-score and share their self-assessment in one-on-one scorecard review sessions.

Part II: Clear Expectations

People desire and crave structure. This starts in early childhood as children begin to understand routine and predictability. At my center, our toddlers and two year olds actually clap as a collective bunch twice per day without teacher initiation. Once is when they see the meal cart being rolled into the classroom for lunch and the second time is when the lights come on after naptime. Now it's not likely that your teachers will clap and celebrate you rolling the lunch cart around, but providing structure subconsciously supports every person's desire to feel safe which is the primary need on Maslow's Hierarchy.

Clarity, consistency and specificity are three of the most important things when setting clear expectations. This requires that the leader of an organization make the expectation clear for themselves first. Once you're ready to communicate expectations to staff, be sure to provide the what, how, and why. Also be prepared to communicate expectations multiple times, in multiple ways, including both verbally and in writing.

Developing a standard operating procedures guide is a timely process but when procedures are in 'black and white', very little is left to be misunderstood. Be sure that such a guide is easily accessible by staff and not done simply to meet a licensing requirement. An easily accessible guide also gives staff a reference point and ensures that they don't have to rely only on memory, especially since there are so many important points for members of your team to grasp.

The final step in communicating expectations is to get agreement and commitment from employees that they understand and agree to follow the expectations. Their written signature provides evidence of training and is useful if you ever face any legality incidents such as having to appeal unemployment.

One final note on expectations. It is okay to have different expectations for different people on your team. There are some members of my team that I expect to simply meet expectations while there are others that I expect to score a level 4, and surpass and exceed expectations. In a world that values fairness, this can be a controversial statement. Nonetheless, if we really are to develop people to their full potential, as their leaders, we have to be okay with pushing some people harder than others. This means that every now and then, you'll need to have the, "I expect more from you because..." conversation. The communication here is the key. If communicated clearly and in advance, many of your employees will not only accept the difference, but also embrace them.

Out of the Box Idea

My favorite tool for reinforcing expectations is our weekly news note. This is a quick half sheet of paper that outlines our quality focus for the week and includes quick reminders, staff shout outs related to our core values, due dates, and any special activities for the week.

The bottom two lines include a space for responding to the following, "This week, I'd like the following resources/support...." and "This week, I will demonstrate excellence by...." It is distributed on Monday mornings and staff must review and respond to it and turn it in by the end of the day. This tool is useful to support communication and as a source of reinforcement and retraining.

STRATEGY 6:
Define your Non-Negotiables

One of the best things that you can do for your team is to really get to know yourself as a leader. As a foundational strategy, we discussed the importance of making a list of what you want in an employee. The next thing to get clear on is your non-negotiables. What is it that you cannot and will not accept? These are different from State standards or regulations, and are usually the most critical factor in the smooth operation of your program and subsequently, the foundation for your program's long-term success.

In many business circles, you'll hear company leaders refer to the unwritten rules of success when discussing the advancement of their organization and of their employees. As times changes and millennials create a stronger presence in the workforce, the days of the unwritten are gone. Yes, you actually need to write the rules! In the case of non-negotiables, you'll make a list of the 5 to 10 'rules' that are most critical to the success of the smooth operation of your center.

Non-Negotiables may cover a variety of topics but at minimum should include the following: attendance, leave, and professional responsibilities. I wrote our non-negotiables when I was turning around my company and the middle of what I often refer to as boot camp (because my employees now tell me that I was a drill sergeant during those days). I'm too embarrassed to share them in this book but if you email me, I'll share them with you. At the time, we had several repeat violations and our center literally needed to be in 100% compliance of every last standard. I don't recommend being a 'drill sergeant' unless you're in a similar situation.

Sample Non-Negotiables Topics:

Attendance

Using the Time Clock

Being Prepared / Obtaining Supplies in Advance

Finding Solutions Independently vs. Contacting Director

Turning Lesson Plans in On Time

Using Office Hours

Making Copies of Necessary Forms in Advance

STRATEGY 7: Training and 'Grooming' during Recruitment

Many child care owners and directors don't commonly take advantage of the opportunity to immerse potential employees in their company's culture during the recruitment process. Establishing a positive employee culture starts with the first touch point that you have with a potential employee which for most of us is an online job ad followed by an email or phone call to set up a first round interview. More often than not, we're so busy and afraid of being short staffed that our mission is to get the person in, instead of getting the right person in - the right way.

Now more than ever, program leaders have to examine their workplace culture and provide a clear explanation of why their program is a great place to work. Creative job ads, career pages on your program's website, and email marketing to potential candidates are all ways that programs can communicate their culture before an employee even begins their first day of work.

At our center, we use multiple methods to communicate the culture including posting video testimonials from current staff members online as well as emailing recruitment newsletters to all applicants who have applied highlighting the best things about being on our team.

Strategy Action Steps

- Create a job ad that captures the personality of your organization.
- Create a standardized Email (and automate when possible) thanking employees for their application and outline your procedure for following up. Conclude with a piece of content that highlights 'why you're a great place to work'.
- Create a standardized Email to invite candidates for an interview. Conclude with a second piece of content that highlights 'why you're a great place to work'.

- Provide a welcome letter to applicants once they arrive for the interview. Be sure the letter includes a section outlining what it takes for an employee to be successful on your team.
- Provide a mini-orientation during the interview that mentions your non-negotiables as well as how you take care of your employees.
- Create an interview assignment - I like to have applicants use the back of the welcome letter and respond to the question, what do you think it would be like to work here? What makes you a good 'fit' for our program? This forces them to consider whether or not they fit and also gives you an opportunity to assess their writing skills. As an alternative, you may ask candidates to send you an email with the same response if they are actually interested. Those candidates who are most interested tend to send their emails right away while others may send them in a day or two later, if at all.

Strategy 8: Interview for "FIT"

As an early childhood leader, "what" you hire is based on position - a lead teacher, a curriculum specialist, a program cook, however, the more important piece is "who" you hire, an honest person, a team player, someone who enjoys having fun. Once you've understood this, the recruitment strategies on the previous pages become all the more important.

If you're going to hire for character, your interview structure may need to be adjusted. During our first round interviews I always begin by stating that the primary purpose of the interview is to get to know the candidate as an individual and that their education and experiences in the classroom will be assessed down the line. I usually end with a preview of what it will be like to work here. My speech typically goes like this, "I want you to know that this is a stressful place to work. I try to take really good care of my teachers but they give 110%. I invest a lot in my people [insert examples here] but I always expect a return on my investment." These few lines help potential employees know exactly what to expect if they decide to join our team. Regardless of how much you share or don't share, it's important to know exactly 'who' the person is that you plan to bring on to your team.

Sample Questions

- Tell me about yourself.
- What are your dreams?
- What stresses you out?
- Tell me about the best day of your life.
- If you had to plan a team outing for us, where would we go and why?
- When's the last time you made someone's day?
- If you won an award today, what would it be for?
- What are you looking for in a company?
- What questions do you have about what it would be like to work here?

STRATEGY 9:
Orientation Includes Culture

A comprehensive employee orientation is one of the greatest weapons for preventing issues with conduct and producing culture champions for your program. Unfortunately, many leaders of child care programs use the orientation primarily as a welcoming tool that only scratches the surface on training new employees on the culture. Orientation is not a checklist, a paperwork meeting or a simple review of expectations. Rather, employee orientation is a process that helps new employees assume a new identity as a member of your team. The key to a great employee orientation is to set the tone both in terms of the workplace environment as well as your leadership style while also showing new employees where they will fit within the environment.

One of the greatest challenges when it comes to new hire orientation is timing. There may be some occasions where you are not available to lead orientation or you need a new hire in the classroom right away for ratio purposes. Google slides is a free tool that allows you to create an orientation presentation that can include both content, photos, and videos with the added bonus of quizzes to check for understanding. The great thing is that you can set the quizzes to score automatically and be emailed to you. Once created, new hires can complete this portion of the orientation from any laptop or tablet with internet access.

Strategy in Action

Review your Employee Orientation and be sure that it includes:

1. The Story of the Company History
2. The Story of the Leader
3. Review of MIssion and Vision
4. Training on Core Values

Out of the Box Idea: Smiles, Smiles, Smiles

One of our lead teachers joined our team after working for an Amusement Park in Florida. In order to emphasize the importance of smiling and maintaining their core value of projecting positivity to their visitors, they used a mirror as the cover page of all of their orientation manuals. We've modified that idea and end our orientation with a two minute smile competition where our new hires all sit in front of a mirror and practice holding their smile for two minutes. It's a silly and fun exercise but it has been effective in communicating just how important our core values are to us!

STRATEGY 10:
The Orientation Packet

If you're like me and come from the classroom, you've probably heard the term 'check for understanding'. As a middle school math teacher, I learned that I could spend an entire week on a concept only to find out at the end of the week quiz that my students had not fully grasped what I had worked so hard to teach them. Employees are no different. It is possible for employees to sit through your orientation and training, and miss out on key concepts. For this reason, you need to check for understanding. An orientation packet is a great tool to help you do this.

Orientation packets are simply a folder of assignments for new hires to complete by a certain due date. An orientation packet may include some classroom specific training but should primarily be used to get to know the new hire while also making sure they understand key point about your culture. Since all of your new hires won't actually read your handbook, you may want to include a quick review of key policies. The orientation packet may also include a quality checklist for the new hire to use as a self-assessment in preparation for their first observation by the Director. The other great thing about orientation packets is that they often require new hires to communicate with current employees as they work to complete each assignment. For example, a task in the pack may ask your new hire to complete the hand-washing process while a lead teacher observes them and then have the lead teacher sign off. This helps to introduce your new hire to the systems and procedures within your program and also helps to promote a sense of team collaboration.

Part III: Teachers are Leaders

If we take a brief look at Maslow's Hierarchy of Needs for example, much of the research shows that millennials entering the workforce, who were raised in relative peace and prosperity, are one of the first generations who were raised from childhood to adulthood with the first three levels of Maslow's Hierarchy being taken care of. Their physiological needs as well as their needs for safety and security won't be their focus when taking on employment. Instead, their needs are in the areas of esteem and self-actualization. These include things like personal growth, recognition, and a sense of achievement. This means, when they consider employment, they'll want to know, "What's in it for me?"Some may assume that they're asking this question out of selfishness but in all actuality, they are asking the question with both pureness and confidence because at the core, they are looking for their needs in the areas of esteem and self-actualization to be met.

This is in direct contrast to previous generations who were looking for their biological, physiological, and safety needs to be met. Employees of this generation found satisfaction with basic job security. However, do not assume that because their initial focus is on basic needs that they are uninterested in growth, esteem, and self-actualization.

Regardless of which generational cohort you manage as the leader of your child care program, you'll benefit by assuming a 'Teachers are Leaders' philosophy. At its base, this philosophy recognizes that teachers have some natural desire to lead. If we think about it, teaching in itself requires leadership as teachers assume responsibility for the children in their care, plan and make decisions each day. By giving teachers additional responsibility, you help promote their natural desire to lead and ultimately, push them up Maslow's Hierarchy supporting their self-fulfillment needs and goal of achieving their full potential.

Strategy 11:
Define your Leadership Team

"You are a leader." I probably said this line 1000 times when working on shifting my culture. One of the most common mistakes directors and owners make is giving an employee the title of Lead Teacher and not expecting them to lead. In most programs, lead teachers are responsible for leading the classroom and although the handbook says they are responsible for supervising assistants and aides throughout the day, there is no follow up to assure that this is happening. In order to implement a 'Teachers are Leaders' philosophy, the program director needs to actually define your teachers as leaders. They should be referred to as leaders, treated as leaders, and expected to conduct themselves as leaders and models for the school. When this happens, you're able to delegate several responsibilities (which we'll share in the next few pages) while also creating a culture of growth and advancement. Here are some ways that you can distinguish your teachers as leaders:

- Leadership Meetings: Usually about once per month or whenever we have something big going on, I meet with my team of lead teachers. Leadership meetings are usually about 15 minutes in length and provide an opportunity to check-in with them and disperse information. If you have tablets in your classrooms, there are several free tools that allow you to video conference which is an option that allows everyone to meet while also maintaining coverage. When staffing levels allow, we meet in person usually in the form of a stand-up meeting in the hallway during the naptime/lunch break hour. Regularly scheduling these meetings support collaboration, sharing of ideas, and allow a moment to reinforce to your teachers that they are in fact, leaders.

- Benefits for Leaders: As you develop your teachers as leaders philosophy and cultivate your team of lead teachers, there may be some fringe benefits offered to lead teachers that are not offered to assistants and aides. For example, lead teachers in our program typically earn larger performance based merit bonuses and have additional opportunities for obtaining leadership training. It is a mistake to believe that these additional benefits for lead teachers will lead to division or jealousy. If you believe that this will happen, I encourage you to reexamine your core values and ensure that your staff embodies the values you've set for your program.
- Leadership Training: Effective leadership is a combination of the right qualities and the right training. If you are going to give your teachers leadership responsibility, remember to also provide leadership specific training in the areas of time management, communication, delegation, accountability, feedback, and documentation.

Strategy 12: Leadership Responsibilities

In helping your Lead Teachers assume responsibilities as leaders for your program, there are several tasks that they can be assigned. When we think about assigning tasks, we often shift away from the idea to avoid being a burden or giving them "too much work". We encourage you to keep Maslow's Hierarchy in mind and consider the sense of achievement that is offered when a teacher completes a "leadership" task. The task does require more energy from staff but it also connects them with the company's "big picture" which often makes the additional work more meaningful.

- Program Tours: Whether your program is completely full with a wait list or building enrollment, it is helpful to have teaching staff lead tours. This is a great way to distinguish yourself, save time as a Director, and begin the relationship building process between parent and teacher. In our program, our tours are scheduled at the same time each day. The tour concludes by dropping the prospective family off in the office with the director for additional Q&A.

- Interviewing and Making Hiring Recommendations: As we shared in the previous pages, interviews are one of your most important jobs and offer a great opportunity to introduce prospective employee's to the workplace culture at your program. Allowing your teachers to lead interviews is an organic way to further communicate the culture to the candidate for hire. In order to train your employees on conducting interviews, it helps to have them start by sitting in on interviews and taking notes. Be sure to ask them for their opinion on a candidate and whether or not the person would 'fit' within the established culture.

- Running Errands/Inventory Management: When you have the proper coverage, it is a great habit to permit your teachers to run errands on behalf of the school. In addition to acknowledging your trust in them, this also is a time saver for program directors and owners. If your program doesn't have the flexibility for teachers to leave the building, consider giving your teachers responsibility for placing orders for necessary supplies. Several online retailers allow teachers to submit orders that can be reviewed for approval by the center administrator before the order is finalized.

Strategy 13: Teacher Led Training

As a child care leader you may already have your teachers train new hires as part of the onboarding process. Under the Teachers are Leaders philosophy, teacher training goes to a whole new level. Following the train the trainer model, lead teachers have the opportunity to train others on their team based on new information acquired through professional development opportunities such as conferences. For example, if you send your teachers to a local training, they would take notes and then represent the information in the form of a presentation to their colleagues. Believe it or not, there are some teachers who have been working in the field for years but have never had the chance to prepare presentations or speak before a group of their colleagues. I can tell you firsthand that this strategy will push your staff out of their comfort zone but the sense of achievement that they gain after presenting to their team is well worth the effort.

Strategy 14: Event Planning

Company events are a great way to boost morale and build a positive culture. Some of our best events have been created, planned, organized, and implemented by employees. Program leaders have the option of asking for a volunteer to take the lead or simply assigning the role to a member of the team. In our program, we have staff complete a proposal and request a budget (if necessary). I personally give very little guidance and refer them to Google or colleagues when they come with how-to questions. At the mid-way point of the planning period and at the end, I provide feedback. For our team, this helps to promote a sense of achievement and confidence.

Event Ideas

- Holiday Parties
- Spirit Week
- Class Picnics
- Open House
- Back-to-School Night
- Parent Workshops

Event Proposal

Submission Date: __________ Proposed Event Date:__________

Description of Event: ______________________________________

____

____

Purpose of Event: ____

Proposed Participants: ______________________________________

Materials Needed: ____

Other Needs: ____

Budget Requested: __________ Signature:___________________

Strategy 15: Personal Development for Leaders

One of the first books I read when turning around the culture at my center was *The Dream Manager* by Matthew Kelly. I think about this book at least a couple times per month in my efforts to offer personal development to my leadership team. Personal development offers great benefits to individual staff but also to your team as a whole. It creates a momentum in the workplace to propel both your people and your company forward. In the words of Henry Ford, "If everyone is moving forward together, success takes care of itself."

- Goal Set, Together: To support personal development, it's important that you know the goals that each member of your team has. There's an added benefit of you sharing your goals with them in return. This creates a bond and promotes an empowered culture of individuals who are invested in each other's success.

- Exposure to Life Skills Training; Life skills training is a great addition to the benefits that you offer staff and a great news is that there are a ton of free resources to share. Typically our staff have goals of building their credit score, purchasing a home or vehicle, budgeting or living a healthier lifestyle. We've been able to bring in representatives to lead lunchtime workshops in each of these areas at no cost. In return, we allow the representative to leave promotional material in our staff lounge or hang a small flyer on our community board for parents.
- Build in "Growth Time": All early childhood professionals ranging from the cook to the director serve as caregivers but sometimes self-care for caregivers is a forgotten concept. As a standard, we schedule 3 in-service days per year where our entire team receives one full day of training. During each of these days, at least 90 minutes is spent on personal development time where the exercises and activities are designed to support personal growth rather than professional skill building.
- Cultivate Transferable Skills: One of the most valuable assets to your program will be an employee with transferable skills. Transferable skills are those skills

that are useful in multiple areas and applicable to industries beyond early education. Typically, new staff join us with some 'soft skills' but providing additional development of those skills creates well rounded employees that benefits child care leaders. It can be a bit uncomfortable to think about preparing staff for the future but keep in mind that their future may still involve you.

Strategy 16: Employee Uniforms

Uniforms are one of the most popular ways to build culture within your program. Early childhood is one of the only service industries that doesn't take advantage of this tool. Employees who wear company uniforms generally identify more strongly with their company as a whole, including the company's vision, mission, and core values. As a result, they may feel increased responsibility in upholding those principles and representing the company in a positive manner. Uniforms also promote a sense of pride and confidence (both listed on Maslow's Hierarchy) and reinforce the employee's identity as a member of your team. Additional benefits for your program provided by uniforms include:

- Brand Professionalism: Customers tend to associate company uniforms with large, well established companies. This image bolsters their confidence in a company's professionalism and skills and may serve as a subconscious means for marketing and boosting enrollment.

- Brand Consistency: Uniforms offer the added benefit of providing consistency and consistency sells! The human brain likes consistency and when customers can rely on having the same experience with your program, a sense of trust and reliability is created - both of which are key in the child care industry.
- Brand Expertise: Company uniforms give employees specific authority in the eyes of the customer. Customers tend to view employees in uniform as experts in their field. This opinion increases their confidence in the employee's competence and ability to meet their needs.

Be mindful about providing uniforms as an employee benefit as the cost can quickly add up, especially for items that are branded with your logo. To avoid this, you can choose a specific colored top and bottom that employees are responsible for obtaining and wearing daily.

Part IV: Accountability

What you expect, but more importantly what you accept matters. A key component to any workplace is including accountability within your organization's culture. In its purest form, accountability is taking responsibility for what happens in an area where you have authority. If any organization is going to be successful, everyone has to be accountable for their actions. In other words, everyone has to be committed to fulfilling their responsibilities. A culture of accountability takes things a step further and means that everyone holds everyone accountable. In a field where we are literally responsible for lives, this is even more critical, especially considering horror stories of abuse and neglect that have been media headlines in our industry. At its core, a culture of accountability means, "If you see something, say something." This applies to the new hire who may have on the wrong uniform, an assistant teacher who's taking short cuts on the sanitation methods or even a program leader who isn't fully following a procedure. Team members at all levels should be comfortable with holding each other accountable for the good of the program in its entirety.

Accountability does not mean reporting someone to a supervisor every time something goes wrong. There is value in peers correcting each other, coaching each other, and providing each other with direction and feedback. In order for this to happen, staff need clear guidelines as well as appropriate training in the chain of command. Under the Teachers are Leaders philosophy in our program, lead teachers are the first line supervisors, followed by program managers, and then finally the center director. Program leaders should remember to be consistent to prevent employees from bypassing this structure.

One key point in accountability is to be prepared to extend consequences. Consequences are not punishment, rather, they serve as tools to prevent a behavior from reoccuring. In setting clear expectations, it's important to make clear that consequences do exist and establishing this point in advance, makes administering consequences less tense.

The final point about accountability is to be consistent. Enforcing expectations is an everyday task and when you ignore a policy being broken, staff begin to think that the policy is void, which often causes others to break the policy. This doesn't mean we knit-pick every little thing but acknowledgment does make a difference.

Strategy 17: Classroom Observations and Quality Inspections

As owner, I conduct quality observations at my center periodically which consist of a list of standards and two columns: meets expectations or needs improvement. One of the quality observations is related to implementation of curriculum and support of child development and the other is a basic room inspection for safety and cleanliness. I calculate scores as a percentage and share each classroom's score with everyone on our team after the inspection. I also average the scores to calculate a single score for the entire school. This serves two purposes. First, teachers know exactly what they need to change and know who they can go to for support, based on scores, which promotes collaboration. Second, teachers are able to see how our school is performing as a whole. We know that we're only as strong as our weakest link so if we see that one of our classrooms is struggling, we (meaning both program leaders and staff) can give them our collective support. As a perk, we celebrate with a team reward, often lunch but sometimes a small bonus, if all classrooms get 100%.

Strategy 18:
End of Month Report

A key part of creating a culture of accountability is communication. End of month reports are a great method for communicating and checking in with staff without organizing a formal meeting. End of month reports are a single form that is due at the end of every month. You may have staff complete room inspections or simply complete a reflection of the month. For our program, we have a reflection exercise at the bottom where staff acknowledge at least one person on the team, highlight the biggest challenge of the month and have a box for requesting support. Teachers submit the form to their director who can follow up if necessary.

Strategy 19: Staff Meetings

Staff meetings are a necessary part of building culture. It's rare that an entire team of early childhood teachers can join together in one room due to ratio requirements which means getting together can be a real treat. In order to get the most out of the meetings, program leaders should plan for structured two way communication. Our center, for example, always includes open floor time during the meeting. During this time, teachers are able to communicate the expectations which in some ways is even more powerful than a director or owner doing so. When a teacher says, "everyone needs to be on time" or "we all need to clean-up after ourselves", your culture really shines.

One frequent question is how do you get staff members to attend your meetings. This goes back to clear expectations. During our interviews, one of our questions will be, "We have meetings once per month from 6:15 until... and you'll be expected to attend. Will this be an issue?" If you're concerned that your veteran staff won't attend, you need to go back to your core values and ensure that they are the appropriate fit.

Strategy 20: Retraining Forms

The remedial action form is a great tool for leaders who find difficulty in managing consequences. The form is a written document that requires employees to summarize a situation and include their initial understanding in the area and their new understanding in the area. It doesn't require a lengthy, time-consuming discussion with the employee, staff simply are given a copy to complete and turn in by the end of the day. We use this form for minor incidents or for retraining new employees during their probationary period.

Strategy 21: Rethink Progressive Discipline

Disciplinary action is a term used to describe an employer's responsibility for correcting a pattern of misconduct or a severe disregard for program policies. This can be one of the most challenging areas for child care program leaders, particularly those who are uncomfortable with confrontation. Accountability requires some form of confronting staff members on their actions, however, it should not be done in a demeaning way. In addition, there are instances when a consequence may be necessary for preventing future issues down the line.

Rethinking progressive discipline is an effective way to reinforce the value of your work environment and culture. From time to time you may have staff members who have a disregard for a minor policy. If the disregard was intentional, you may benefit by imposing a mini-suspension in which the staff member is sent home for the day. Instances where this may be appropriate include violation of cell phone policy, intentional misrepresentation of core values, disrespect to colleagues, etc. One reason mini-suspensions are so effective is because they send a message to other employees and also impact employees financially. The key to remember is that you have options beyond imposing a verbal warning. If you are progressing through verbal warning, written warning, counseling, etc. and an employee's behavior is not changing, your progressive discipline policy is not effective in correcting performance.

Strategy 22: Recognition and Rewards

Employees want to love their work and they also have a desire for their contributions to be acknowledged. In order to maximize the effectiveness of your recognition and rewards program at your center, you need to consider the experience that is provided. Sometimes it's not *what* we do but rather *how* we do it, that makes employees feel valued. In other words, employees are often looking forward to the thought behind a thing. As you share your appreciation for your employees and recognize their hard work, consider your core values. For example if one of your core values is fun, do you share recognition in a fun way? At my program, I often use mystery boxes to build excitement around tangible rewards. Sometimes there's a classroom resource in the box but other times the box is holding a gift for the teachers. Taking the extra step to cover the box with gift wrap and allowing teachers to tear it open really goes a long way. As a bonus, you can capture the experience on video to share on your online platforms.

Avoid the pitfall of establishing a formal program that is not clearly understood by employees. This happens commonly with Employee of the Month programs. Often these programs are ineffective due to the lack of a clear formula of how this recognition is earned. Your staff may know that a certain teacher earned an award but may not know the specific strategies that they can take to earn the award themselves. Employees who do not understand how an award won't strive to earn the award which in itself is a motivation killer.

One final note about rewards and recognition. For some program leaders, giving rewards to employees can be disheartening when employees don't respond in an appreciative manner. You may need to communicate the story behind the tangible reward before giving it to employees and actually remind staff to say thank you, particularly if this is something that you struggle with. It's important not to let a perceived lack of appreciation prevent you from sharing rewards with your team.

Free and Low Cost Recognition Ideas:

- Thank You Card
- Thank you Letter
- Certificate of Appreciation
- Shout Out in the Newsletter
- Posts on Social Media
- Stickers
- Share a Compliment Journal

Other Ideas:

- Performance Bonus (with letter)
- On-the-Spot Cash Awards (award publicly)
- Invitation to Lunch
- Mobile Spa Day
- Game Time

Strategy 23: Self-Assessments

An employee self-assessment is one of the best methods to engage employees in the process of looking at performance and setting goals for the future. The self-assessment promotes a healthy workplace culture by encouraging accountability around the assessment standards. In addition, standardizing the assessment clearly communicates what the program director is looking for from child care program staff in regards to performance.

Self-assessments can be used formally but it's also helpful to use them when performance improvements are necessary which may be prior to the annual evaluation. Providing a copy of the assessment prior to the annual evaluation period helps to create self-awareness around strengths and areas of improvement. Self-assessments should be comprehensive and include standards on general work habits, performance in the classroom, and contributions to the team - all of which are integral to a healthy employee culture.

Strategy 24: Employee Surveys

Employee surveys are a vital part of maintaining a healthy culture. They are one of the most powerful mechanisms for formally getting raw and honest feedback. As a best practice, allow employees to submit surveys anonymously and provide both quantitative and qualitative questions. The quantitative questions will provide you with a way to measure progress over time and quickly identify trends while the qualitative questions help to explain outliers. Google Forms is a free tool for creating your anonymous survey and allowing your staff to submit their feedback online.

Tips for Increasing the Effectiveness of Employee Surveys

1. Encourage Participation
2. Maintain Confidentiality
3. Share Results with Staff
4. Act on Results and Provide Progress Updates

Part V: Fun & Appreciation

As you work to build a positive culture for your child care program, it is important not to forget the fun. When fun is consistently infused into the work environment it can boost morale, decrease absenteeism, and help your staff to avoid employee burnout. You'll find that as your team embraces an attitude of joy and enthusiasm, a positive energy will be created that will be felt throughout the workplace. When working to figure out just how fun your workplace is, ask your staff for their thoughts and ideas. We typically include this on our employee survey but you can also bring up the question in general conversation. Also, remember that your role as a leader requires you to be enthusiastic and participate in the fun. Your staff will never be more enthusiastic than you are so be prepared to step out of your comfort zone and set the example for your team.

Strategy 25:
Use of Surprise and Anticipation

Imagine waking up for work feeling uninspired, tired and hoping for the day to be over before it starts. You finally get to work and BOOM, It's employee Zumba Day. When your reality doesn't meet your expectations, the positive experience of shock can affect you like no other. In fact research shows the nucleus accumbens, one of the 'pleasure centers' in the brain, to be much more active when individuals experience surprises. In other words, surprises bring us pleasure. Likewise, anticipation of a positive experience also creates a pleasurable experience in individuals. Research from Robert Sapolsky, a neuroscientist highlights that the feel good chemical dopamine is released from the brain in anticipation of a reward. Many people think that dopamine is released when the brain receives a reward, but dopamine is actually released in anticipation of a reward. Notably, twice as much dopamine was released in his experiment when unpredictability and anticipation were a factor (https://www.psychologytoday.com/blog/brain-wise/201510/shopping-dopamine-and-anticipation).

As a child care leader, you can begin to use anticipation and surprise very easily. For example, if you are going to buy breakfast for staff, print a quick message and let staff know that they can expect a BIG surprise in the morning for their hard work. If you're doing a staff outing, consider having staff sign up to visit a "secret location". In 2015, when I was working to shift our employee culture, I planned a team outing to the County Fair about 45 minutes away. Our teachers followed my car and had no idea what we would be doing until we actually arrived. Imagine the surprise of seeing goats, pigs, cows, and even bears upon entering the fairgrounds. Two years later, we still laugh about this. It's all about creating experiences (and memories!) for your team.

Strategy 26: Child Centered Events

Think way back to the days of primary school. Can you remember your favorite day? Maybe it was a visit from the Fire Department, the 100th day of school celebration, a field trip, or even field day. Whatever it was, I'm sure it brings back many warm memories. Now, imagine the memories created for your teacher on this special day. Perhaps, your favorite day as a child was just as special to your very own primary teachers.

Child centered events are those special days that you create in your program just to make children smile. These events are a hit for children and families but also staff. Depending on your program arrangements and state ratio requirements, this may be one of the only times when your entire staff can experience an event together. In addition, these special events often provide opportunities for your teachers to tap into their inner child. For example, our program plans a field day at the end of each summer. We have several games for children but the event always ends with a teacher relay that involves hula hoops, dancing, and water balloons. This is a great way to end the summer on a high as you prepare for the Back-to-School season. We recommend planning events at least once per month, keeping in mind that there are several ways to plan events at no cost to your program.

Plan <u>FREE</u> Events for Every Month of the Year		
January	Measure your Feet Day	Visit from Local Shoe Store Staff (Ask them to bring their tool and measure children's feet after reading a story. Share the information with parents to ensure they are buying the correct shoe size).
February	National Children's Dental Health Month	Visit from Local Dentist
March	National Reading Month / National Music Month	Visit from Local Librarian
April	Financial Literacy Month	Visit from Local Banker

May	National Bike Month	Bike Day at School
June	National Safety Month	Visit from Local Police Department
July	National Postal Service Appreciation Month	Visit from Mail Carrier
August	*National Senior Citizens Day:*	*Visit from Local Seniors or Grandparents*
September	National Good Neighbor Day:	Invite Neighbors who Live or Work near your Center to Read a Story
October	Fire Safety Month	Visit from Local Fire Department
November	National Good Neighbor Day:	Visit from Local Military Personnel
December	Eat a Red Apple Day	Visit from Local Produce Manager at Grocery Store

Also remember to celebrate milestones such as your center's anniversary, teacher birthdays, and work anniversaries with the children in your program. Once events are planned, you may consider doing a monthly school calendar which is a great tool for marketing just how great your program is to both current and future parents.

Out of the Box Idea: School Partnerships

Consider reaching out to your local middle school and high school special elective departments to see if they may be interested in partnering with your school for special events. For example, consider asking the music teacher if they might consider bringing their students on a field trip to perform for your children. This scenario is usually a win-win as your program gets a free performance and their students get an opportunity to practice performing for a small crowd.

Strategy 27:
Team Outings

Have you ever heard the saying, a team that plays together, stays together? If you haven't heard it, it's a good time to consider an outing for your staff. Team outings are different from on-site team building activities as outings provide a change in scenery and help eliminate distractions. Often the new environment helps your staff to overcome personal barriers or barriers associated with workplace politics or hierarchy. Regardless to what activity you plan, outings help to promote team skills and provide a sense of employee appreciation, especially when the outings are designed for fun.

One of the most common questions from child care leaders relates to how they can increase participation in team events. Here are some tips:

- Have a teacher plan the outings.
- Offer an incentive for participating.

- Make eligibility for bonuses contingent on participation in team events.
- Make your outing fun. Remember the release of oxytocin will help the brain relax.

Out of the Box Idea: Market your Team Appreciation

Moms and Dads just want to have fun! A great way to distinguish your program for prospective parents is to share just how committed you are to maintaining a positive employee culture and taking care of your team. Team outings provide great photo and video materials that can be used in your email marketing or social media campaign. In an industry that is riddled with parents who want a center with low turnover, teacher appreciation really goes a long way.

Strategy 28: Team Competitions

Door decorating competitions, spirit week outfits, and even attendance competitions can all be useful in giving your employees a boost in their morale. Competition impacts employee culture by motivating your team to work together to achieve a common goal. You can get parents involved by allowing them to vote or consider involving your tours in on the fun by encouraging them to vote on some of the visual competitions.

You'll find that some teachers are super competitive while others may be resistant to participating. If you're not comfortable with making participation mandatory, consider giving out raffle tickets to participants and choosing the competition winner based on the number on the raffle ticket that is selected at the end of the competition. This will allow the focus of the competition to be on participation rather than being the best.

Out of the Box Idea: Staff Only Spirit Week

The fun continues next week as we take stage with our cast spirit week:

- Monday: Hat Day!
- Tuesday: Twin Day!
- Wednesday: Dress like your favorite Book Character Day!
- Thursday: 80s Day!
- Friday: We're rolling out the red carpet for.... Dress like a Queen Day!

Participation is Required By All

Strategy 29: Time for ME!

"Surprise", take the rest of the day off for yourself. That's what I call R&R&R, relax, reflect, and refresh. There's nothing like a boss who cares and giving your employees some time for themselves goes a long way in creating a healthy culture within your company. If you're really going to build a great team, individual well being amongst your employees should be a priority. It is important to note that you may not be able to offer a full-day off so instead of offering a mental health day, consider offering a mental health hour which allows employees to come in later, leave earlier, or take a longer break. This is particularly helpful in the winter months which is when we often see increased signs of burnout in teachers of all ages. Studies show that providing this time away from the work environment as an employee benefit helps increase retention and productivity.

To ensure that you consistently provide 'me-time' for employees (and yourself!), it can be helpful to schedule on the calendar a few months in advance. This helps with planning and also helps your staff to have something to look forward to. Also, consider giving your teachers a self-care checklist (like the one below), to help them make the best of their time off!

To:

Enjoy Time for **YOU**!

1. TAKE A BUBBLE BATH
2. DEEP CONDITION YOUR HAIR
3. APPLY A FACE MASK
4. TURN OFF YOUR PHONE
5. SEE A MOVIE
6. LIGHT A CANDLE
7. PAINT YOUR TOES
8. WRITE IN A JOURNAL
9. TAKE A DEEP BREATH & PUT THINGS IN PERSPECTIVE
10. LISTEN TO YOUR FAVORITE SONGS
11. GO FOR A DRIVE
12. HAVE YOUR FAVORITE DESSERT

Thank you for **all you do** to make our school a special place!

Strategy 30: Themed Weeks

We've all heard of Teacher Appreciation Week and most of us take time to go out of our way to make sure that our teachers know just how much they are valued. The week usually ends with a ton of smiles, cards, and gifts to carry home. This should not be the only time per year that we fill our teacher's buckets with appreciation. Consider planning activities for additional themed weeks where you can take time to pour in to your teachers. Financial literacy, self-care, and employee wellness are just some ideas that you can implement to help support your staff's personal development. Some other popular themes are community spirit week, colleague appreciation week, and core values week. You can find many free curriculum ideas online and build an entire employee engagement ideas to help promote a positive workplace culture.

Examples of Themes to Implement with your Staff
Financial Literacy Curriculum Ideas
• Celebrate "Money Mondays" by passing out free finance resources and articles. • Provide a template for employees to create a budget. • Encourage employees to visit www.annualcreditreport.com to obtain their credit score. • Provide employees with a list of free spending tracking apps or websites. • Invite a representative from your local bank to lead a workshop at lunch time for staff.
Employee Wellness Curriculum Ideas
• Celebrate "Wellness Wednesdays" by passing out free wellness resources and articles. • Obtain free trial passes from your local gym or fitness center and distribute to staff. • Host a mini field-day at lunch time or after-work for employees. • Pass our sleep tracking logs and have an 8 hours of sleep challenge. • Create a wellness wall to share healthy recipes, exercise routines, and wellness progress.

Part VI: Parent Culture

If you really want to build a positive culture for your employees, it is important to have a strategy for parent culture as well. The families that you serve play a huge role in your school community and have a direct impact on employee culture. Building a positive parent culture starts with creating policies for your families and consistently implementing these policies fairly amongst all of your parents. When considering policies, we encourage you to have a clause that outlines your expectation for parent conduct behavior. For example, our client-center agreement states that we reserve the right to immediately terminate care for behavior by parents that is considered disruptive or discourteous to any member of our team or our school environment. This clause helps to set the tone for positive conduct within your school community. The second part of building a positive parent culture requires you to engage them and provide opportunities for them to get involved and feel a part of your school community.

Out of the Box Idea: Family Photo Wall

Photos are a great way to build a sense of community throughout your school. A family photo wall can be a big hit for children and parents alike. Some time towards the end of their first month, we snap a picture of parent and child at pick-up or drop-off. We print and laminate two copies - once goes on the wall and one goes home to the parent with a thank you card for choosing our program.

Strategy 31: Parent Council

Establishing a Parent Council is a good way to give your parents an outlet for sharing ideas and concerns regarding your program. Parent council can allow you to delegate work to families such as door designs, bulletin boards, cutting, copying, event planning, etc. In some cases, you may also be able to take advantage of your parent's areas of expertise and connection to others in the community. Finally, parent council can help you visualize your center from a parent's perspective and provide benefits similar to a focus group.

To ensure that the council remains a positive experience for your school, it is helpful to establish a clear purpose and meeting norms, otherwise you risk the chance of creating a power struggle between the center leadership and the parents. To form a parent council, you may ask specific families to join or give families the opportunity to sign up. Be sure to provide a consistent time and place to meet and share the time commitment requirement before families agree to participate.

Sample Parent Council Mission

The mission of the parent council is to:

A. Promote activities that enhance the joy and well-being of our center's students and staff in a way that complements and enriches the school's mission and philosophy;

B. Build community within the school, and enhance the relationship amongst the school's teachers and parents and the wider community.

C. Provide a collaborative forum for families, administration, and teachers of our school to share ideas and feedback on program policies and initiatives.

Strategy 32: School Parties

Everyone loves a party. Since parents typically only experience your early childhood program during pick-up and drop-off, they may not have a full idea of just how awesome your center is! Center-wide celebrations are a perfect way to build school pride and a sense of community, both of which are helpful for maintaining a positive culture.

One of our most successful events was our Infant Family Paint & Sip. Families were provided apple cider and set in a circle in our infant classroom painting with their babies on blank canvases. The relationships formed at this event have followed from our infant classroom all the way to our preschool classroom. Photos from the event also provided awesome marketing visuals.

If your school celebrations are focused on community building, consider doing an ice breaker or assigning an event host to help promote socialization amongst families.

School Party Ideas

Costume Parade

Character Celebrations (related to books)

Holiday Parties

In-House Field Trips (Clown, magician, reptile guy, concerts, etc.)

Anniversary Celebrations

Classroom Play

Classroom Concerts

Strategy 33: Collaborative Events

There's no better place for a parent to bring out their inner kid than their child's early childhood program. Allowing parents to roll up their sleeves, get messy or participate in a silly activity is an awesome way to promote a happy and healthy culture. Collaborative events are a great idea and include any opportunity for teachers and parents to work together. They give your parents the opportunity to feel more committed to your program and create a sense of belonging so that they can feel like partners with your program rather than customers. Collaborative events also help to break the monotony of the daily routine and serve as a morale booster for your staff.

When we refer to collaborative events, we're referencing events that require both teachers and parents together for a common goal. Some goals may be for a formal cause such as fundraising while others are less formal and just give the two parties an opportunity to interact in an informal way. Our toddler teacher organized a hula-hoop competition for Dads at the end of summer picnic. If you can imagine the fun shared as our Dads hula-hooped to the chicken song after a long day's work. These types of events give families the opportunity to build connections and strengthen their relationship with your staff and will also change how they respond to issues that may potentially arise in the future.

Collaborative Events

Field Day / Outdoor Games

Sports Competitions

Volunteering Together

School Supply Drive

Canned Goods Drive

Out of the Box Idea: Moms vs Teachers

Each year our program organizes a Moms vs Teachers competition. The competition is held on a Saturday in the Fall and up to 15 Moms compete against our team of teachers on a two hour photo scavenger hunt on our community Main Street. Teams receive a free t-shirt branded with our logo to support marketing efforts. We meet at the local pizza place for lunch at the conclusion of the competition.

Strategy 34: Parent Workshops

When most directors consider providing educational workshops to parents, they forget to tap into their most valuable asset - their teachers. Allowing teachers to plan and lead workshops for parents helps to build on the trusting relationship between teacher and parent while also branding your teams as child development experts. Teachers already know the children well and so they'll be able to provide targeted information that will be of great value to parents. Giving teachers this opportunity also helps to develop their leadership skills and helps to build their confidence and esteem.

Workshops are also a great way to build a sense of community within your program. It can be an empowering realization for parents when they realize that other families may be dealing with the same challenges that they are.

Sample Parent Workshop Topics

Responding to Challenging Behaviors

Routines and Transitions

Setting Limits with Love

The Power of Choice

Promoting Positive Peer Interactions

Strategy 35: Over-Communicate

If you ask both teachers and parents, what's one thing that your child care program can improve on, many times the reply is communication. Many child care program directors depend on a parent board and monthly newsletter to share communication about the program, however, this is not enough. The principle of over communication means communicating the same messages in multiple ways, including directly and indirectly. This goes a long way to prevent confusion, misunderstanding, and even disagreements for parents in your child care program and is a necessary part in maintaining a healthy culture within your program. Many leaders may avoid this principle because they believe that over communication will somehow bother their customers. The truth is that your parents and customers want to know all about you and what is going on within your program.

- Consider adding a weekly Email to your program that provides a quick overview of the week. The increased communication helps highlight all of the great things that your program is probably already doing.
- Monthly Activity Calendar
- Verbal Communication from Teachers
- White Boards on Classroom Doors
- Event Flyers

Strategy 36:
Grab & Go

Setting up a grab and go station is a great way to show appreciation to the parents you serve. Typically once per month we roll out the breakfast cart, place a note of appreciation above the cart just to say thank you to our parents. This is a relatively low cost activity which may include, bananas, breakfast bars, donuts, or, fruit, or bagels. You may also provide coffee or orange, many of the main chains places will provide free cups.

As you build relationships with other small businesses in the community,you may also consider cross promotion marketing. For example, you may consider partnering with a local coffee shop or cafe to provide some of the grab and go items in exchange for their business cards being placed at the grab & go station or photos on their social media page. If you do not have any food services businesses nearby, consider reaching out to small businesses in other industries to sponsor the monthly grab & go, such as a children's clothing store, pet care business, or local spa or salon. As an added bonus, if your staffing allows, consider having a teacher present to hand out the grab & go items as this is a great way to build parent-staff relationships outside of the four walls of the classroom.

Strategy 37: Make Parents Feel Needed

Making sure your parents feel needed will be an important part of your child care business. People crave connection and as you work to develop a sense of community, you build their trust in your program and help to promote their confidence and self-esteem as they take on an active role within your center. One way you can make sure your parents feel needed is to provide opportunities for parent involvement. Since your program may serve busy working parents, opportunities should vary in nature and range the spectrum of commitment. In addition, involvement tends to increase when multiple invitations to get involved are offered including one-one request from program directors and teaching staff.

Parent Involvement Ideas

- **Mystery Readers**: A parent visits the classroom as a surprise and spends 15 minutes reading 1 or 2 short books.
- **Talent Committees**: Parents can sign up to do bulletin boards, door decorations, or update center displays.
- **Take Home Projects**: Setup a volunteer box near the entrance with grab bags that include a take-home project such as laminating, letter tracing, cutting, etc.
- **Field Trip Chaperones**: Parents join the classroom to help supervise and engage with children on field trips or during special in-house activities.

Be sure to show your parent volunteers appreciation in order to keep them involved. In addition to personalized thank you cards, consider framing a photo as a keepsake of their involvement in your program. Publicly recognizing volunteers can also be a way in which you can let your parents know you value their help. Providing a shout out in the center newsletter is a great tool for public recognition.

You may also consider creating a photo wall of fame which is a great highlight for current parents and prospective families who may be visiting your program for a tour.

Strategy 38: Parent Survey

In order to maintain a positive parent culture, you need to regularly survey parents. It's helpful to conduct your survey at the same time each year prior to any major transitions in order to get the most relevant feedback. In addition to feedback, surveys also offer your families a safe place to vent any concerns or frustration in a private space. This can be useful in preventing them from sharing these concerns on a public review site online, particularly if they know that there is an opportunity for a quarterly or semi-annual survey in advance of a problem.

Google forms is a free tool for creating a survey to distribute online. Once you create the questions, you can send a link for families to complete the survey anonymously or you may give them an option to include their name for a follow-up call from program management. Remember to always set a specific timeframe they have to get it completed so that you get answers and all questions or concerns addressed and fixed in a timely fashion.

Family Survey Instructions

Step 1: Create survey questions. Be sure to include questions that can be quantified as well as open ended questions that parents can respond to.

Step 2: Email an invitation to complete the survey and provide up to a 10 day deadline for families to complete the survey.

Step 3: About half-way through the survey period, provide an update on the number of responses and what your goal is. Be sure to remind families of how the survey will be used.

Step 4: Send a final reminder the final day of the survey.

Step 5: Within 14 days, be sure to provide a summary of the responses to staff and parents. Be sure you outline your program goals based on the feedback received.

Strategy 39: First Names

Addressing parents by first name makes parents feel comfortable and it helps build parent teacher relationships. It makes them feel important and happy that you remember their name. In addition, it creates a level of respect and sense of partnership between the parent and teacher. Learning first names of parents can be a challenge for staff, especially those who are new to your team. Consider having parents complete about me sheets and making these available to staff, or at a minimum having name sheets available for staff to refer to.

When staff refer to parent's by name, most often, the parent's level of interest in getting to know the staff member also increases. Their sense of comfort with that particular caregiver may also increase which promotes trust and confidence in your program.

Final Thoughts

I hope that this book adds value to your leadership journey in the early childhood education field. Building a positive culture is not only critical to leading a successful team, it is critical for leading a successful life. In other words, as your culture improves so will your life and the lives of those who support your program.

Happy Culture Building!

About the Author

Stephanie Harris can be described as driven, highly energetic, and passionate about leadership. At just 26 years old, Stephanie opened her first business in 2014, meeting her lifelong goal of opening a childcare center. Five years later, Stephanie owned her second location. Since opening her centers, Stephanie has gone on to provide over 300 hours of professional development to early childhood teams as a leadership and organizational culture trainer and consultant.

Check out our guided journals on Amazon

Business Meetings with God by Stephanie Harris

Planning Time with God by Stephanie Harris

We invite you to connect with Stephanie online in the Facebook group 'Child Care Empowered' at www.Facebook.com/groups/ChildCareEmpowered

or

visit www.ChildCareEmpowered.com

Dedicated to my Mom, Judith Harris and my grandparents Ralph and Maxine Harris. Thank you for giving me the foundation that I needed to live my dream!

Made in United States
Orlando, FL
24 March 2022

16110220R00072